# When CESAR CHAVEZ
## Climbed the Umbrella Tree

by Rachael Hanel    illustrated by Alex Herrerias

PICTURE WINDOW BOOKS
a capstone imprint

Young Cesar Chavez spotted a poor, hungry man near his house. "Please come to my home. My mother has food for you," he said.

The Chavez family had been through hard times too. But Cesar's mother, Juana, believed sharing was important. She often sent her children out to look for the poor or homeless. She said to Cesar, "What you do to others, others do to you."

Cesar would grow up to fight for people who needed help. He knew what it was like to move from place to place, work long hours, and sometimes not have a place to live.

3

Cesar Chavez was born March 31, 1927, near Yuma, Arizona. His parents were Librado and Juana. They had come from Mexico to the United States. Aunts, uncles, and cousins lived nearby. Family was very important.

The Chavez family owned a country store and pool hall near their home. They also farmed the land there. Cesar helped care for the farm animals. He also helped to run the store and pool hall.

4

After chores, Cesar and his five siblings rode horses and swam in the canal in front of their house. The children loved climbing a big cypress tree they called The Umbrella Tree.

"Look at me!" Cesar yelled. "Look at how high I can go!"

After the sun went down, people gathered behind the Chavez home. Adults told stories about farmers in California. Cesar and his brother Richard listened. They dreamed of the places they could go and the things they could do. Anything was possible.

The Chavez children went to school near their home. When Cesar started school, he did not know much English. But English was the only language allowed in class. Students were punished for speaking Spanish.

Cesar sat next to his older sister, Rita, for a few days, instead of joining the other kids in his class. He felt safe with his sister.

At bedtime, Juana gave her children lessons. She told stories about helping people in need. She had tales about bad children who got into trouble. She wanted her children to help others and to be kind. "You always have to help the needy, and God will help you," she said.

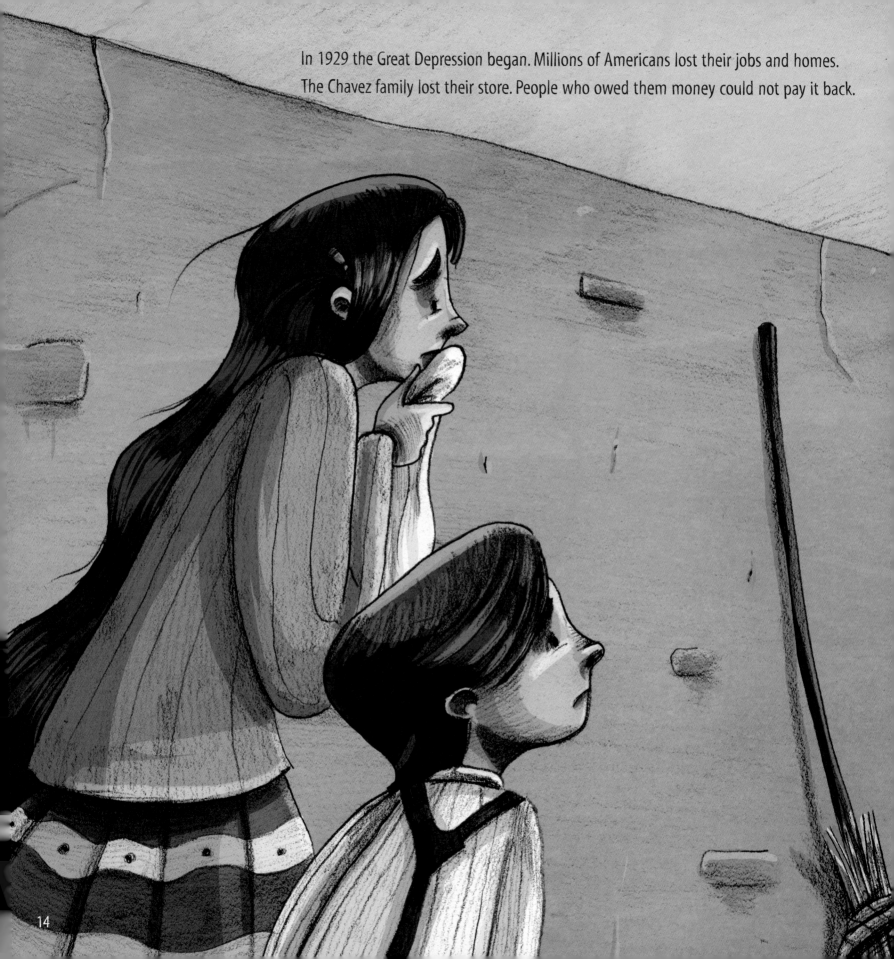

In 1929 the Great Depression began. Millions of Americans lost their jobs and homes. The Chavez family lost their store. People who owed them money could not pay it back.

Cesar's family still had the farm. For a while it seemed like they would be OK. But the family's debts piled up. Cesar's father left home to find work.

In 1939 the family had to leave the farm. Cesar watched as the new owner plowed over all of his favorite spots. All the places he and his brothers and sisters loved were gone.

The Chavez family, along with thousands of other migrant workers, went to California. They went from farm to farm to plant and harvest crops. Everyone, including children, worked long hours. The jobs were hard, and they paid very little. Cesar and his family sometimes lived in farm labor camps. Other times they slept in tents or under bridges.

Although he had to work hard, Cesar found ways to have fun. On special occasions, he and his brother Richard walked to the movie theater. They watched *The Lone Ranger*. At home the boys listened to boxing matches on the radio. They liked the famous fighter Joe Louis.

As teenagers, the boys went to dances and learned steps like the jitterbug.

When Cesar and Richard wanted extra cash, they went through the trash. Cigarette packs had small pieces of tinfoil inside. It took a very long time, but they once gathered enough tinfoil to create an 18-pound (8.2-kilogram) ball. They sold the foil and bought shoes and clothes.

Being the new kid at school can be tough. Children of migrant workers had an even harder time. They were often made fun of because they were poor and did not speak English well. Cesar's sister Rita dropped out of school when she was just 12 years old. She loved to learn but was embarrassed to go to school without shoes.

Because the family moved a lot, Cesar went to many different schools. One day a teacher came to find Cesar. She asked him why he was behind in school. She was sad when she learned that he was missing class to work. Cesar liked that she cared enough to ask about him. He never forgot her kindness.

Cesar finished eighth grade in 1942. He was 15. But then his father, Librado, was hurt. Cesar quit school to work full-time. He wanted to help his family. He took jobs picking fruits and vegetables. He shined shoes for extra money.

One time Cesar tried to buy a hamburger at a diner. The staff there said, "We don't sell food to Mexicans."

"I'm not Mexican! I'm American!" he wanted to shout. He thought it was unfair that he couldn't buy a hamburger just because of the color of his skin.

Cesar never forgot the challenges and injustices his family faced as migrant farmworkers. He wanted people to know that their thoughts and feelings mattered, no matter what their jobs were. **"Farmworkers are not agricultural implements or beasts of burden to be used and discarded,"** he said.

UNFAIR TO FARM WORKERS!

# Afterword

Cesar was a young boy when he started hearing about unions. In a union, workers join together to ask for better treatment. They might agree to stop working and go on strike. They could form a picket line to prevent others from going to work.

But by the early 1960s, working conditions for migrants on California farms had not improved. Children were forced to work and miss school. Adults were paid low wages, or sometimes not even paid at all. Workers suffered from being in the sun all day. Many did not get enough to eat or have decent places to live. Chemicals used to fight bugs or weeds made them ill.

In 1962 Cesar, Dolores Huerta, and other fellow activists founded a union. It became the United Farm Workers of America. In 1965 Latino and Filipino grape workers demanded fair wages and better treatment. Farm owners did not want to meet their demands. So the grape workers walked out of the vineyards on strike, refusing to work. The owners sometimes used threats and violence.

Cesar encouraged striking workers to fight back peacefully. He asked them not to work at grape farms on strike. In 1966 Cesar led a 300-mile (483-km) march in California, from Delano to Sacramento. He helped the striking workers travel across the nation to tell people about their low wages and bad working conditions. Cesar also asked people not to buy California grapes. By refusing to buy grapes, ordinary people could support the union.

By 1970 Cesar's hard work began to pay off. Because people supported the boycott of grapes, the union was able to get workers better wages, benefits, and treatment at work. What had started as a small movement became a big success. When Cesar died in 1993, more than 45,000 people attended his funeral.

# Glossary

**agricultural implement**—machinery used in farming

**canal**—a channel that is dug across land; canals join bodies of water

**debt**—something that is owed

**farm labor camp**—living spaces provided by government agencies, growers, or others for migratory or seasonal farm labor

**Great Depression**—the years from 1929 to 1939, when there were few jobs in the United States and most people had little money or food

**injustice**—an unjust act

**jitterbug**—a kind of dance step that includes swinging and twirling in patterns

**migrant farmworker**—a person who moves from place to place for work, such as harvesting or planting crops

**occasion**—a special or important event

**picket line**—a group that is formed when workers decide to stop working to demand better wages or better hours

# Read More

**Carlson Berne, Emma**. *What's Your Story, Cesar Chavez?* Cub Reporter Meets Famous Americans. Minneapolis: Lerner Publishing, 2016.

**Meachen Rau, Dana**. *Who Was Cesar Chavez?* Who Was . . . . New York: Grosset & Dunlap, an imprint of Penguin Random House, 2017.

**Roome, Anne Ross**. *Cesar Chavez: Champion for Civil Rights*. Rookie Biographies. New York: Children's Press, 2016.

# Critical Thinking Questions

1. Name two ways in which Cesar Chavez's family influenced him to fight for the rights of farmworkers. Use examples from the book as your evidence.

2. Name two traits that helped Cesar become a successful leader. Support your answer with examples from the text.

3. Cesar could have remained angry after his family lost the farm, and when the waitress refused to serve him a hamburger. Explain how those moments may have inspired him.

## Index

## Internet Sites

Use FactHound to find Internet sites related to this book.

Visit *www.facthound.com*

Just type in this code: 9781515830429 and go!

Super-cool stuff!

Check out projects, games and lots more at
**www.capstonekids.com**

# Other Titles in This Series

When **Amelia Earhart** BUILT A ROLLER COASTER

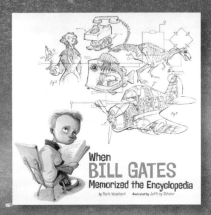

When **BILL GATES** Memorized the Encyclopedia
by Mark Weakland
Illustrated by Jeffrey Ebbeler

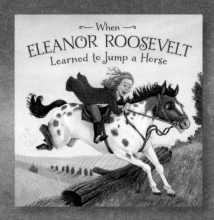

When **ELEANOR ROOSEVELT** Learned to Jump a Horse

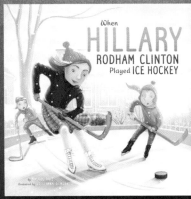

When **HILLARY** RODHAM CLINTON Played ICE HOCKEY

When **Martin Luther King Jr.** WORE ROLLER SKATES

When **NEIL ARMSTRONG** Built a Wind Tunnel
by Mark Weakland
Illustrated by Luciano Lozano

When **ROSA PARKS** Went Fishing
by Rachel Ruiz
illustrated by Chiara Fedele

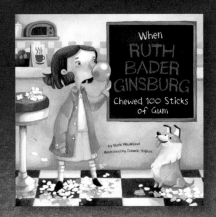

When **RUTH BADER GINSBURG** Chewed 100 Sticks of Gum
by Mark Weakland
illustrated by Daniele Vaglian

When **THOMAS EDISON** FED SOMEONE WORMS
by Mark Weakland
Illustrated by Thomas Radcliffe

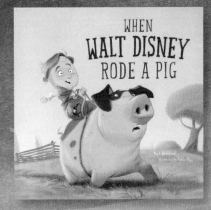

When **WALT DISNEY** RODE A PIG

When **Wilma Rudolph** Played Basketball
by Mark Weakland
Illustrated by Daniel Duncan

Special thanks to our adviser for his advice and expertise:
Marc Grossman
Spokesman
Cesar Chavez Foundation

Editors: Mari Bolte and Shelly Lyons
Designer: Ashlee Suker
Creative Director: Nathan Gassman
Production Specialist: Tori Abraham
The illustrations in this book were created digitally.

Editor's Note: Direct quotations are indicated by **bold** words.

A direct quotation is found on the following page:

p. 26, line 3–4: Hofrichter, Richard. *Toxic Struggles: The Theory and Practice of Environmental Justice.* Philadelphia New Society Publishers, 1993, p. 167.

Picture Window Books are published by Capstone,
1710 Roe Crest Drive, North Mankato, Minnesota 56003
www.mycapstone.com

**Cataloging-in-publication information is on file with the Library of Congress**.
ISBN 978-1-5158-3042-9 (library binding)
ISBN 978-1-5158-3051-1 (paperback)
ISBN 978-1-5158-3055-9 (eBook PDF)

Summary: Cesar Chavez is famous for his role as a civil rights leader. But do you know what he was like as a child? From losing his childhood home to toiling in fields as a migrant worker, Cesar wanted to help. This playful story of his childhood will help young readers connect with a historic figure and will inspire them to want to achieve greatness.

Printed and bound in the United States of America.
002306